THE CHRISTIAN'S CREED
A WORKBOOK

Becoming Rooted in Christ, Established in the Faith

By

Stanley D. Gale

Waxed Tablet Publications

This workbook is designed for use with
The Christian's Creed: Embracing the Apostolic Faith
(Stanley D. Gale, Reformation Heritage Books, 2018).
Quotations are used by permission.

© 2020 by Stanley D. Gale
ISBN 978-1-67819-313-3

Special thanks to Rebekah Olson
for giving this workbook its visual appeal.

Not Just a Study Guide

This workbook carries a dual purpose.

One, it serves as a study guide for *The Christian's Creed: Embracing the Apostolic Faith*. Through questions, interactions, and observations it draws out the major points of each chapter and explores the biblical underpinnings of the declarations of the Apostles' Creed. Some questions will be straightforward; others will get the wheels turning to think through the substance, structure, and flow of the Apostles' Creed.

Two, the workbook not only directs our study of *The Christian's Creed*, it also engages the God featured in the Apostles' Creed itself, the triune God of our salvation. In his letter to the church at Rome, after laying out the glories of a God-orchestrated salvation, Paul erupts in doxology (Rom. 11:33-36). Likewise, we will respond to God for who He is and what He has done as we work our way through the Apostles' Creed.

Ultimately, the purpose of this workbook is captured in Colossians 2:6-8 – that we might be rooted and built up in Christ Jesus the Lord, and established in the faith, protected from a false gospel.

Be sure to read the appropriate chapter in the book before undertaking the corresponding lesson in the workbook. In the workbook "Creed" will refer to the Apostles' Creed, while "book" will refer to *The Christian's Creed*. Ask the Holy Spirit to guide your study.

NOTE TO LEADERS. You will not find a Leaders Guide edition of this workbook with the answers filled in for two reasons. One, leaders need to have read, reviewed and wrestled with the areas covered to equip them to lead others in discovery. Two, to give "the" answer stifles perspective and promotes mechanical response. People often take note of different things and express them in different ways. Drawing out insight enriches discussion, ultimately enhancing appreciation for the faith summarized in the Apostles' Creed.

CONTENTS

The Apostles' Creed

I believe in God, the Father almighty,
Maker of heaven and earth.

I believe in Jesus Christ, his only Son, our Lord,
who was conceived by the Holy Spirit
and born of the virgin Mary.
He suffered under Pontius Pilate,
was crucified, died, and was buried;
he descended into hell.
The third day he rose again from the dead.
He ascended into heaven
and is seated at the right hand of God the Father almighty.
From there he will come to judge the living and the dead.

I believe in the Holy Spirit,
the holy catholic church,
the communion of saints,
the forgiveness of sins,
the resurrection of the body,
and the life everlasting. Amen.

Preface

As you therefore have received Christ Jesus the Lord,
so walk in Him,
rooted and built up in Him and established in the faith,
as you have been taught,
abounding in it with thanksgiving.
Beware lest anyone cheat you through philosophy and empty deceit,
according to the tradition of men,
according to the basic principles of the world,
and not according to Christ.
(Colossians 2:6–8)

Have you ever walked through a swamp? At night!

You have to be very careful where you step. Your flashlight needs to be pointed to the ground. Even when you find a patch of solid ground to put your foot, you need to test it first to make sure it will hold you.

That is what it's like for us in the world we live. The Bible calls it a *fallen* world. It is filled with dangers and misdirection. But God gives us His Word, the Bible, as a light to our path and a lamp to our feet. Its beam cuts through the thick darkness to show us the firm foundation for our steps. By it, God Himself takes our hand to guide us.

Complicating things are false teachers who give us wrong direction. They say, "This is what is good and right and true," or "This is the way of life; follow me." On some occasions what they say seems right and makes sense to us, but the Bible warns: "There is a way that seems right to a man but its end is the way of death" (Prov. 4:12).

That means we need to be attentive not only to our footing but also to our pathway, realizing there are competing walks to life and those that appeal to us may not be the best and may, in fact, be deadly.

The Bible passage quoted above comes from Paul's letter to the Colossians; it sounds a note of warning. It is part of a letter written to a church where false teachers were trying to lead God's people astray. So Paul cautions: "Beware lest anyone cheat you through philosophy and empty deceit, according to the tradition of men, according to the basic principles of the world, and not according to Christ" (Col. 2:8). The word "cheat" can be expressed "take captive" and reminds us that there is a battle for our minds and hearts, orchestrated by the enemy of our souls.

How do we keep ourselves from being taken captive and led astray? God's apostle says we need to be "rooted and built up in [Christ] and established in the faith as you have been taught." Reflect on those words for a moment: rooted, built up, established. They are words that communicate stability and security. This surefootedness to life is gained through *being taught*.

That expresses a basic rule for how we follow Jesus as His disciples. We need to be taught of Him and, upon hearing His word, we need to put it into practice. Jesus said that in His Sermon on the Mount (Mt. 7:24) and He gave that instruction in making disciples when He said to *teach* them all that He had commanded (Mt. 28:18-20).

We become rooted and built up in Christ and established in the faith by being taught. That means we *learn* to know where to step, what path to follow, and how to recognize quicksand by sitting at the feet of Jesus.

In another one of Paul's letters, he tells us that this discernment between truth and error is a mark of maturity. Children tend to be naïve and easily led astray. But being established in the faith will allow us to "no longer be children, tossed to and fro and carried about with every wind of doctrine, by the trickery of men, in the cunning craftiness of deceitful plotting" (Eph.4:14). Teaching will protect us and equip us to deal with spiritual predators.

What exactly are we to be taught? The apostle tells us that we are to be grounded in *the faith*. Our faith is to be in *the* faith. We trust and rest in the sound teaching given by God. The beating heart of that teaching is the gospel of our salvation.

That is what the Apostles' Creed does. It is an ancient statement of faith that summarizes the Bible's teaching on the gospel of salvation that centers on the person and work of Jesus Christ. For generations, God's people have relied on this declaration of belief to give words to their hope of salvation. It lays out in *what* we are to be rooted, built up, and established. The Apostles' Creed was not written by Jesus' apostles but it does reflect their teaching as foundational, so that our faith might be "built on the foundation of the apostles and prophets, Jesus Christ Himself being the chief cornerstone" (Eph. 2:20).

While the Apostles' Creed does protect us from another gospel, most of all it displays the glory of so great a salvation. It brings us to a mountaintop vista of redemption and allows us to behold the panorama of a salvation bound up in the living and true God. It testifies to what *God* – Father, Son, and Holy Spirit – has done for us. Not what we do, but what God has done. That means all the glory goes to God. To study the Creed is like sitting before a masterpiece in an art museum, except it is not just to be studied and admired; it is be believed, taken as one's own through faith, and savored as nourishment to the soul.

In this workbook we will walk through the Apostles' Creed. We will unpack the Creed's content, trace its contours, and follow its flow as it leads from the plan of God in eternity past to the believer's place with Him in eternity future. Our exploration will be guided by a study of the Bible's teaching behind the Creed laid out in *The Christian's Creed: Embracing the Apostolic Faith*.

This workbook is a study companion to *The Christian's Creed* and will ask you to interact with portions of the book. Be sure to read the appropriate chapter before undertaking the corresponding lesson. It is a workbook rather than a study guide in that its purpose is not only to explore the meaning of the Apostles' Creed but also to provoke a faith response to the God whose gospel the Creed captures.

May the Holy Spirit help you in your study. Pray even now toward that end. And as the Spirit leads you, may He fill your eyes with the wonders of God's salvation and fill your heart with fresh awe and love for Jesus Christ.

SDG

Introduction

CONFESSING THE FAITH

Our approach is not to explore the history of the Apostles' Creed and its development in the early church. Rather, we want to understand the declarations of the Creed and take note of the logic with which the declarations unfold. Particularly, we will explore the teaching of the Bible behind the declarations.

Read the Introduction of *The Christian's Creed*.

1. In what way does the Apostles' Creed relate to the apostles?

2. Read Ephesians 2:18-22. The church is said to be built on the *foundation* of the apostles and prophets.

    a. In what way are the apostles and prophets the foundation of the church? (compare Eph. 4:11-14; Heb. 1:1-2)

    b. How many foundations does a building have? What does this say about the finality and sufficiency of the teaching God has given us in the Bible through the apostles and the prophets? (compare 2 Tim. 3:16-17; 2 Pet. 1:3, 19-21)

3. The Apostles' Creed makes it clear that salvation is of the Lord. The Creed divides into three sections, addressing the Father, the Son, and the Holy Spirit respectively. But its emphasis is not so much that God is triune as it is that salvation is Trinitarian – *grounded* in the saving purpose of God the Father, *gained* through Christ His Son, and *granted* by the Spirit of the risen Christ. The Creed lays all the glory of salvation at the feet of God alone. Fill in the blanks to show the role attributed to each Person of the Godhead in salvation.

    The Father _____ salvation

    The Son _____ salvation

    The Spirit _____ salvation

4. What does it mean that the Apostles' Creed communicates the *fundamentals* of the Christian faith?

5. The final paragraph of our book's Introduction says that the Creed is liturgical, catechetical, confessional, and missional. What does each of these mean?

Read the last chapter of our book (Conclusion: AMEN).

1. How does the "Amen" of the Creed relate to "I believe" with which the Creed begins?

2. Which of the purposes of the Creed – liturgical, catechetical, confessional, or missional - does the story of the pastor and the dying man illustrate? Why?

In preparation for the lessons to follow, read aloud the Apostles' Creed on page 5 of this workbook. Read it as *summary* of *the* faith. Read it as an *expression* of *your* faith. Ask the Holy Spirit to guide your study, to lead you into all truth, to give you understanding that you might be rooted and built up in Jesus Christ and established in the faith.

What questions do you have after reading the Introduction and the Conclusion to *The Christian's Creed*?

Chapter 1

A STAND OF FAITH

I believe.

The first line of chapter one of our book claims that the words, "I believe," can be "life shaping, direction changing, and risk taking." Can you think of any examples where this is true? If not, ask those who entrusted themselves and their life savings to men who promised great reward but who were later exposed for their Ponzi schemes. To all appearances these men were legitimate, trustworthy, and full of promise, but turned out to be frauds and false hopes for financial security.

Who and what we believe in carry consequences.

Belief is another word for faith. Faith in something means we trust it and we entrust ourselves to it.

I BELIEVE

The writer of Hebrews gives us a meaningful definition of faith: "Now faith is the substance of things hoped for, the evidence of things not seen" (Hebrews 11:1).

1. How does this definition describe faith as the opposite of wishful thinking?

2. Why does "unseen" not mean "unreal"? What realities does faith see?

3. Read Hebrews 6:17-20. What is the anchor of Christian hope?

4. Read Hebrews 12:1-2. How does faith relate to Jesus?

5. What is the connection between faith and hope?

6. According to 1 Thessalonians 5:9-10, what is the ground for Christian hope? How is this reflected in the Apostles' Creed?

WHAT IS TRUTH?

The Christian faith invites belief because it consists of truth. In John 18:33-37, Pilate is interrogating Jesus. Jesus says that He bears witness to the *truth*, and those who are concerned with truth will listen to Him. To that Pilate asks, "What is truth?" (John 18:38).

Jesus never answers, or at least John does not record an answer. Our chapter suggests no answer is given because John's *entire* Gospel account answers Pilate's question. John uses words like *testimony* and *witness* and *truth* to build the case for Jesus as the Christ. His account holds evidentiary value for the purpose statement of his Gospel: "These are written that you may believe that Jesus is the Christ, the Son of God, and that believing you may have life in His name" (20:31). John's goal is to persuade the reader to embrace Jesus by faith.

1. In what way does the Apostles' Creed call us to recognize, affirm, and embrace truth?

2. If the Creed draws boundaries of truth by what it declares, that means there is teaching *within* those borders and teaching *outside* of the borders. What does that say about what we are to believe? (see Col. 2:8)

3. Some will acknowledge that Jesus is the way, the truth, and the life while others will say there are other ways to come to God for salvation. What's the problem with this?

BELIEVING THE CREED

1. What does it mean to *believe* the Creed?

2. Why do even mature believers need the Creed?

3. The Creed invites personal commitment when it calls for personal faith (I believe). What is special about being with others who take up the same words and make the same commitment of personal faith together in a worship service (I also believe)?

4. Explain how the Apostles' Creed is each of these:

    A summary of faith

    A statement of faith

    An expression of faith

    A refresher of faith

THE WEIGHT OF FAITH

The last paragraph of Chapter 1 begins with these words: "Belief is not part of the Creed, but it is what, by God's grace, activates it for personal salvation." What does this mean and how is it illustrated by the dynamite blasting cap in the paragraph prior?

We are the ones who believe but the *ability* to believe for eternal life comes from God. How does John 1:12-13 show this? (Compare Eph. 2:8-9)

Read John 20:28-29. If we have not seen Jesus as Thomas did, what is it we are to believe? (Compare Jesus' story in Luke 16:19-31, especially the last verse.)

Turn your eyes to God right now. Ask Him to help you understand the truth of His Word. Ask Him to open your eyes to behold Jesus, to gaze upon the glory of God in the face of Jesus. Pour out your heart to Him in trust and thanks and praise.

What questions do you have after reading Chapter 1, "A Stand of Faith," in *The Christian's Creed*?

Chapter 2

THE GOD

I believe in God.

*Without faith it is impossible to please Him, for he who comes
to God must believe that He is, and that He is a rewarder of those
who diligently seek Him. (Heb. 11:6)*

Have you ever heard someone speak of the value of believing in a
higher power, something beyond themselves? Some invite you to
believe in a god as you *imagine* him (or her) to be, perhaps a god well
suited to meet your needs and circumstances. What is the drawback in
believing in a god you imagine?

The Bible makes it very clear there is only one God, and that we are to
gain our understanding of Him through what He has told us about
Himself in the Bible. It is important that we acknowledge this one God
and give Him the glory due His name.

1. What do these passages tell us about God?

    Psalm 139:1-16

    Psalm 96:1-5

    Psalm 90:1-6

2.   What tendency does Romans 1:18-25 identify in each of us?

3.   How are believers described in 1 Thessalonians 1:9 in respect to God?

4.   How does the expression "living and true" help us distinguish the God of the Creed from idols or the gods of people's imaginations?

THE GOD

Read Acts 17:16-34

1.   (vv. 22-23a) How did Paul know the people were religious? Verse 23 suggests *worship* is part of being religious. What might people worship (1 Thess. 1:9; Rom. 1:25)?

2.   (v. 23b) Was Paul being arrogant to think his understanding of God was better or more accurate than the people of Athens? Where did Paul get his ideas about God? What would you say to someone who told you, "My god is not like that!"?

3. (vv. 24-25) How does Paul describe God that might surprise his audience?

4. (vv. 26-28) What are some of the ways Paul points out that God relates to those He made? How do these ways honor God and humble us?

5. (v. 29) What error in understanding God does Paul correct in this verse?

WHAT GOD?

1. Why does the Apostles' Creed begin with declarations about the Father rather than beginning with Jesus?

2. What can we learn from Paul's approach with the religious thinkers of Athens for our sharing the gospel with others?

3. What are some ways people gain their conceptions about God?

4. How does John 3:14-17 show that the God of the Old Testament is the same God of the New Testament?

GOD AND THE GOSPEL

1. In what way can our understanding of God affect our
    understanding of the gospel?

2. How do God's wrath and love relate to each other to help us
    understand the work of Jesus Christ in the Creed?

When God calls people to *repent* (Acts 17:30), He establishes two things.
One, that He has authority over those made in His image. Two, that
there is a rebellion of heart that people must turn from in seeking God.

Repentance was a regular feature of the response to Paul's gospel
message. In Acts 26:20 he says that repentance should show up in a
changed life. Peter, in the first proclamation of the gospel message in
the book of Acts, also calls for a response of repentance (Acts 2:38).

1. What does it mean to repent?

2. Thinking of our tendency noted in Romans 1:20-23 and
    considering Paul's message to the philosophers in Acts 17,
    what might we repent of?

THE GOD OF THE CREED

God has always existed. He is uncreated, without beginning and without end – infinite, eternal, and unchanging in all that He is. He is separate from what He has made. He is not limited by space or time, or dependent in any way like we are (see Ps. 139).

The God of the Bible is the God of the Creed. The Creed takes us from the purpose of God the Father, through the purchase of God the Son, to the pursuit of God the Holy Spirit.

The Creed has a flow from top to bottom (e.g., Matt. 27:51, Phil. 2:5-8, John 15:26-27). It unequivocally displays not what we do or did, but what God has done and does. That means that all glory, honor, and praise belong to God and God alone.

Open your Bible to Psalm 145. Use these inspired words to lead you in prayer and praise to such a great God. Reflect on each aspect. Linger. Like you might be awed by the overlook at a national park, let this vista of God's glory and grace fill your gaze and lift your heart to the God it honors.

What questions do you have after reading Chapter 2, "The God," in *The Christian's Creed*?

Chapter 3

FATHER AND MAKER

I believe in God, the Father almighty,
Maker of heaven and earth.

From eternity there is only one God, existing in three Persons – Father, Son, and Holy Spirit. While the Son (Col. 1:15-17) and the Spirit (Gen 1:2, 26) are identified along with God the Father (Neh. 9:5-6) as author of creation, the Apostles' Creed points us to the Father who sent His Son.

1. How is this role distinction among the Trinity relating to salvation seen in John 17:3-5?

2. By what two phrases does the Apostles' Creed introduce us to God?

3. Read the verse below from Hebrews 11, which deals with faith. Why do you suppose the first article of faith for the writer of Hebrews has to do with God as *Creator*?

   By faith we understand that the universe was created by the word of God, so that what is seen was not made out of things that are visible. (Hebrews 11:3)

4. What tone does the Apostles' Creed set by beginning with faith in God in relationship to and with His creatures?

RELEVANCE AND REVERENCE

1. In what way does the opening of the Apostles' Creed stir us to worship?

2. Read the quotation from Robert Rayburn in our book. For what two things is God to be worshiped?

3. What does it mean to worship God?

4. Why is God alone to be worshiped?

5. Read Psalm 100 and describe how it inflames and instructs our worship.

Our chapter speaks of the credentials for God cited by the Apostles' Creed as bringing us to "holy ground on holy business." How does this imagery impact our expectations in studying the Creed?

MAKER OF HEAVEN AND EARTH

The apostle Paul begins his explanation of the gospel to the church at Rome by exposing the basic sin of mankind. Read the text below and explain what exactly that sin is.

For since the creation of the world His invisible attributes are clearly seen, being understood by the things that are made, even His eternal power and Godhead, so that they are without excuse, because, although they knew God, they did not glorify Him as God, nor were thankful, but became futile in their thoughts, and their foolish hearts were darkened. (Rom. 1:20–22)

In Romans 1:18, Paul says that people "suppress" the truth about God they see in the world God has made. That language suggests that people don't just ignore the truth; they actively deny it.

1. How do we see denial of God in popular thinking today?

2. What does it mean to acknowledge that God is maker of heaven and earth?

3. How is declaring the faith of the Creed the opposite of suppressing the truth?

4. Why is acknowledging God as the Creator important for embracing the gospel of our salvation?

Pause now to pour your heart out to God using the words of the psalmist.

I will lift up my eyes to the hills—from whence comes my help? My help comes from the LORD, Who made heaven and earth. (Psalm 121:1–2)

THE FATHER ALMIGHTY

This phrase of the Apostles' Creed weds two concepts about God that we affirm by faith. We tend to associate God's might with creation. We survey the sprawling universe and we stand in awe of the power of our God. But the Creed ties God's might with His fatherhood.

1. What encouragement can we find in knowing God not only as our Heavenly Father but as the Almighty?

2. Read the passage below. How does it contrast confidence in the creation with confidence in the Creator?

   What then shall we say to these things? If God is for us, who can be against us? ...For I am persuaded that neither death nor life, nor angels nor principalities nor powers, nor things present nor things to come, nor height nor depth, nor any other created thing, shall be able to separate us from the love of God which is in Christ Jesus our Lord. (Rom. 8:31, 38–39)

3. What confidence does knowing God as Father Almighty give us if we have rested in God's salvation through Jesus Christ? (see John 10:27-30)

God reveals Himself in the Bible by many wonderful names, such as Lord of hosts, Redeemer, Holy, God Most High, I AM, and Judge of all the earth. As believers we get to call God "Father."

1. What does it mean to you to be able to call God "Father"?

2. Read Galatians 4:4-7. What blessings belong to the one who by grace can call God "Father"?

3. According to John 1:12-13 how does a person become a child of God, with all the rights and privileges of that status? (see 2 Cor. 4:6)

4. How would you answer someone who insisted that God is the father of all mankind, and not only of Christians?

Notice that the phrase "God the Father Almighty" occurs in *both* the first and second sections of the Creed. How does this phrase connect the two sections?

Reflect on the following passage from John's first letter and write out a prayer to the God who expresses His fatherly love to you in Jesus Christ.

> *Behold what manner of love the Father has bestowed on us, that we should be called children of God! Therefore the world does not know us, because it did not know Him. Beloved, now we are children of God; and it has not yet been revealed what we shall be, but we know that when He is revealed, we shall be like Him, for we shall see Him as He is. And everyone who has this hope in Him purifies himself, just as He is pure. (1 John 3:1–3)*

What questions do you have after reading Chapter 3, "Father and Maker," in *The Christian's Creed*?

Chapter 4

JESUS THE CHRIST

I believe in Jesus Christ,
His only Son, our Lord.

We've noted that the Apostles' Creed expresses a belief in one God – Father, Son, and Holy Spirit. There are three Persons in one God, existing in eternal communion with one another. There are not three gods. There is one God. This one God is not in three parts but each Person in the Trinity is wholly God, the same in substance, equal in power and glory.

But we've also noted that the primary purpose of the Creed is not to teach the Trinity but that salvation is Trinitarian. The Creed introduces us to this one God working in perfect concert. The Father appoints salvation, the Son accomplishes salvation, and the Spirit applies salvation.

The Apostles' Creed lays out a redemption grounded in the triune God and centered in the person and work of Jesus Christ. So we are not surprised to see that the prominent section of the Creed addresses the person and work of Jesus, commanding more lines than the other two sections combined. The Father provides the way. The Spirit points the way. Jesus is the way.

This focus on the person and work of Jesus is consistent with the charge of Paul to the church: "till we all come to the unity of the faith and of the knowledge of the Son of God, to a perfect man, to the measure of the stature of the fullness of Christ" (Eph. 4:13). Unity of *the faith* is paralleled with unity of *the knowledge of the Son of God*. Central to being established in the faith is being rooted and built up in an understanding of who Jesus is and what exactly He did in carrying out the Father's will.

This lesson helps us to understand Jesus by His titles laid out in the Creed.

THE CHRIST

1. What do the titles *Christ* and *Messiah* mean?

2. What connection do the following passages make between the Old Testament and New Testament about Jesus?

    John 5:36-40

    Luke 24:44-47

3. How is Jesus the One anointed as prophet, as priest, and as king different from anyone in the Bible before Him? (e.g., Heb. 9:11-14)

4. How do the four New Testament Gospel accounts and the Book of Acts make clear that Jesus is the promised Messiah, the Christ of God?

JESUS

1. What does the name *Jesus* mean?

2. Read the birth account of Jesus in Matthew 1:18-25. In what three ways does the birth of Jesus fulfill the prophecy made by Isaiah over 700 years earlier?

3. "Immanuel" speaks to the baby's _____. "Jesus" speaks to the baby's _____.

GOD'S ONLY SON

1. The Creed speaks of Jesus as God's "only Son." That indicates that Jesus is divine. He is *God* incarnate. How do the following demonstrate the deity of Jesus?

   John 9:37-38

   Mark 2:5-7

   John 5:18

   John 8:58

2.   What are the two natures of Jesus?

3.   How do Hebrews 1 and Hebrews 2 show these two natures?

4.   Read 1 Timothy 2:3-6.

   a.   Who is called "Savior"? (v. 3)

   b.   Why is the *humanity* of Jesus emphasized? (v. 5)

   c.   What qualifies Jesus to be the *mediator* between a holy
        God and sinful humanity?

OUR LORD

1.   What does the Creed mean by speaking of Jesus as "Lord"?

2.   As God, Jesus has always had authority. He is sovereign ruler
     over all that He has made. In what sense, then, was Jesus *given*
     authority by the Father? (Matt. 28:18, Eph. 1:20-22)

3. How is this authority seen in Peter's declaration about Jesus in Acts 2:36?

4. What does it mean to refer to Jesus as *our* Lord," as the Creed puts it?

KINGDOM CREED

Jesus taught a great deal about the kingdom. He came to establish a kingdom (Luke 1:31-33). He made it clear that His kingdom was not of this world (John 18:36). His kingdom would be eternal and holy. His saving rule began with His first coming and will be completed when He returns in glory.

1. How do we enter the kingdom? (Mark 1:15; Phil. 2:5-11)

2. From what kingdom are we transferred and how? (Acts 26:18, Col. 1:11-14)

3. In what way is the Apostles' Creed like a pledge of allegiance to the kingdom of God? (Matt. 7:21-23, 1 John 4:1-6)

It is important that we have a clear understanding of Jesus. He is more than an historical figure, more than a good teacher, more than a compelling example. In Matthew 16:13-17 Jesus puts this question to His disciples: "Who do you say I am?" That question is relevant for each of us. What do you believe about Jesus? Turn to Jesus right now in prayer and tell Him what you believe.

What questions do you have after reading Chapter 4, "Jesus the Christ," in *The Christian's Creed?*

Chapter 5

BORN, BLED, AND BURIED

I believe in Jesus Christ...who was
conceived by the Holy Spirit and born of the virgin Mary.
He suffered under Pontius Pilate,
was crucified, died, and was buried;
he descended into hell.

The Apostles' Creed declares, proclaims, reminds and invites us in the knowledge that God saves sinners. As Jonah stated so pointedly: "Salvation is of the Lord." In the Creed, we confess not what *we* do but what *God* has done.

God alone is the author of salvation, something quite clear in the formulation of the Creed. Yet the Creed gives prominence to the person and work of God the Son. Christ is the centerpiece of the Creed. The Father points to the Son at His baptism (Matt. 3) and His transfiguration (Matt. 17). The Spirit points to the Son (John 14-16). While the Creed lays out a redemption grounded in the triune God, that redemption is centered in the person and work of Jesus Christ.

Having looked at the person of Jesus we now want to examine what exactly He did to accomplish salvation. This chapter addresses what is often called Christ's humiliation, His humbling Himself. The trajectory is *down*, from heaven to hell. The next chapter takes us from the grave to glory. Read the portion of the Apostles' Creed quoted at the beginning of this lesson. List the words that describe the downward trajectory.

BORN

Of the four Gospel accounts, only John begins with the pre-incarnate Christ (John 1:1-4). John calls Jesus "the Word" and highlights that He *was* God and was *with* God in His eternal being. This Word became flesh (John 1:14), taking on full and authentic humanity in order to carry out the promised mission of redemption (John 3:14-17).

1. What does "incarnation" mean?

2. Complete this sentence: Jesus was fully _____ and fully _____ in one _____.

3. The writer of Hebrews helps us to understand Jesus' incarnation. Read Hebrews 2:14-17.

    a. What two things does the writer draw our attention to about Jesus' body?

    b. Why was it important that Jesus took on full and complete humanity?

    c. What is significant about the mention of Abraham?

4. How was Jesus' conception different from the miraculous conceptions of Isaac (Gen. 17:15-19 & 21:1-2) and Samuel (1 Sam. 1)?

5. What three reasons are given in our book for Jesus being born of a virgin?

BLED

Christians talk a great deal about the blood of Jesus. Read Hebrews 9:11-26 and 10:4, 11-12, 19. These passages tell us that there is a connection between the blood of sacrificed animals in the Old Testament and the blood of the sacrificed Son of God in the New Testament.

1. What do we learn about the shedding of blood?

2. How was the sacrifice of animals *like* the sacrifice of Jesus?

3. How was the sacrifice of animals *unlike* the sacrifice of Jesus?

4. Why was the sacrifice of animals repeated but Jesus was sacrificed only once?

The Apostles' Creed leads us to follow a path to the grave that includes Jesus suffering under Pontius Pilate.

    1.   Who was Pontius Pilate?

    2.   Why might the Creed mention Pilate by name?

When Jesus arrived at the altar of the cross, He was the unblemished Lamb of God without stain of sin.

    1.   What does it mean for Jesus to be without blemish (1 Pet. 1:18-19)?

    2.   Why was this important?

    3.   What qualification did this give Jesus that we do not have nor could ever have?

How would you answer these questions about Jesus' death?

    1.   Why was it necessary for Jesus to die?

2. Who was ultimately responsible for Jesus' death?

3. How does Jesus' death display the love of God? (see John 3:16; Rom. 5:8-9)

BURIED

The Creed reflects what Paul says in 1 Corinthians 15:3-4 that Jesus not only died but that He was buried.

1. How was Jesus buried?

2. What is significant about Jesus' burial?

The phrase stating that Jesus "descended into hell" was added later to the Creed but reflects something essential to Jesus representing us in our humanity.

1. What is the difference between *Gehenna* and *Hades*, both of which can be translated "hell"?

2. When we die what happens to our body? What happens to our
    spirit? How does the phrase "descended into hell" reflect what
    human beings experience at their death, and what we would
    expect of Jesus as our fully-human representative?

3. What does Hebrews 9:26-28 tell us that Jesus as our
    representative faced at His death?

We have followed Christ's descent from eternal glory with the Father
and the Spirit to His becoming a created being, suffering the
ignominies and miseries of a sin-riddled world, being betrayed by His
foes and His friends, and being condemned to death even though He
was declared "innocent" at trial. He would suffer the physical and
especially the existential horrors of the cross, die, be buried, and
experience the separation of body and soul – and all willingly!

The Bible says He did it out of love (Eph. 5:25). He even found joy
(Heb. 12:2), not in the suffering but in securing His bride, the church,
for Himself (Eph. 5:25, Rev. 19:6-7).

Reflect on these things. Put words to the stirrings of your heart at such
a great salvation and such love Divine.

What questions do you have after reading Chapter 5, "Born, Bled, and
Buried," in *The Christian's Creed*?

Chapter 6

RISEN, REIGNING, RETURNING

The third day he rose again from the dead.
He ascended into heaven and is seated
at the right hand of God the Father almighty.
From there he will come to judge the living and the dead.

Having reached the depth of descent, the Creed now heads upward from the grave to where Christ reigns in glory for His church. This is often called Christ's *exaltation*. It begins with the statement: "The third day he arose again from the dead."

Our book approaches the Creed's statements on Christ's resurrection through two headings: its verdict and its value. Did it really happen and what difference does it make if it did or did not?

THE VERDICT

In his sermon at Pentecost in Acts 2:22-36, the apostle Peter builds a case through laying out four strands of evidence, leading us to the verdict that Christ is risen indeed. List the verses from Acts and the conclusion to be drawn from each strand of evidence below.

The Man

The Plan

Expert Witnesses

Eyewitnesses

1. What closing argument does Peter make in Acts 2:33-36?

2. What should this verdict provoke in us? (Acts 2:37-39)

THE VALUE

In chapter 15 of his first letter to the Corinthian church, the apostle Paul lays out the cardinal tenets of the Christian faith. "For I delivered to you first of all that which I also received: that Christ died for our sins according to the Scriptures, and that He was buried, and that He rose again the third day according to the Scriptures" (1 Cor. 15:3–4).

Paul prefaces this statement by saying this was the message he received and was passing on through preaching. This message of victory offered salvation to those who believed. He will go on to explain that salvation rests on the *reality* of the death and resurrection of Jesus. Jesus truly rose as one actually dead.

There is an interesting picture in the book of Revelation (5:1-6). It is of a throne, surrounded by a diverse multitude of worshipers. On the throne is a live lamb. But that lamb is not just alive; it is alive as *having been slain*. That lamb is a representation of Jesus – crucified, dead, risen, and reigning. He holds the position He does because of His sacrificial death and victory over death.

What Revelation pictures, Paul preaches. Read 1 Corinthians 15:12-19

1. List all the things Paul describes as empty (or vain) if Jesus is not really risen.

2. What does it mean for these things to be "empty"?

3. Why do suppose Paul is so emphatically negative in these verses?

4. What does this say about the importance of Jesus literally being raised from the dead?

Read 1 Corinthians 15:20

1. How does this statement undo all of the "what if" scenarios of verses 12-19?

2. In light of v. 20, write out all the negatives of vv. 12-19 in positive form.

3. How does verse 20 give credence, confidence, and comfort to those who believe for what is described in verses 21-26?

REIGN AND RETURN OF THE RISEN ONE

The Creed speaks of Jesus' ascension, His reign on high, and His return.

   1.   What does Acts 1:6-11 tell us about Jesus' ascension?

   2.   What do the following passages say about Jesus' reign on high, what is often called His *intercession*?

       Romans 8:31-34

       Hebrews 7:23-25

       Colossians 3:1-4

   3.   Jesus reigning on high for us does not mean that He is not with us. What do the following passages say about Jesus being *with* us?

       Matthew 28:18-20

       John 14:15-20

4. How will Jesus' return in glory be different from His first coming to Bethlehem?

5. What contrast does John make in John 12:47 and John 5:27-29?

6. Whether we are alive when Christ returns or have died, what confidence can we have at the judgment if our faith is in Christ? (see 1 Thess. 4:14-18)

Taking an art appreciation course can be an eye-opener. It orients us to things we would not ordinarily note. Paintings often not only depict a scene; they tell a story and so draw us in by the genius of the artist.

For us to truly appreciate the splendor of God's masterpiece of redemption in His Son, we need the instruction of His Word so we can know all the details, and we need the illumination of His Spirit to understand and believe them (1 Cor. 2:13-14).

But even then we continue to grow in appreciation as we study this masterpiece over the course of our lives. Paul's prayer for the believers at Ephesus is essentially a prayer for gospel appreciation. Make this prayer your own.

[T]hat the God of our Lord Jesus Christ, the Father of glory, may give to you the spirit of wisdom and revelation in the knowledge of Him, the eyes of your understanding being enlightened; that you may know what is the hope of His calling, what are the riches of the glory of His inheritance in the saints, and what is the exceeding greatness of His power toward us who believe, according to the working of His mighty power which He worked in Christ when He raised Him from the dead and seated Him at His right hand in the heavenly places, far above all principality and power and might and

dominion, and every name that is named, not only in this age but also in that which is to come. And He put all things under His feet, and gave Him to be head over all things to the church, which is His body, the fullness of Him who fills all in all. (Eph. 1:17–23)

What questions do you have after reading Chapter 6, "Risen, Reigning, Returning," in *The Christian's Creed*?

Chapter 7

THE HOLY SPIRIT

I believe in the Holy Spirit.

Both the Apostles' Creed and the Nicene Creed exhibit a Trinitarian structure, three sections addressing the Father, the Son, and the Holy Spirit respectively. Note, however, the differences when it comes to the Holy Spirit.

"I believe in the Holy Spirit." – The Apostles' Creed

"We believe in the Holy Spirit, the Lord and giver of life, who proceeds from the Father and the Son; who with the Father and the Son together is worshiped and glorified." – The Nicene Creed

1. How would you contrast these two ancient creeds in respect to the Holy Spirit?

2. Why do you suppose the Nicene Creed gives greater description of the Person of the Holy Spirit?

While the two creeds differ in respect to the description of the third member of the Trinity, they go on to follow the same pattern in speaking of the church, the resurrection of the believer, and the prospect of eternal life – all under the heading of the Holy Spirit.

1. Why do these creeds lay out benefits of salvation in the section under the Holy Spirit?

2.   Following our book, how does the Spirit relate to each of the
      benefits listed below?

      The holy catholic church

      The communion of saints

      The forgiveness of sins

      The resurrection of the body

      The life everlasting

SPIRIT OF CHRIST

The Holy Spirit is God, the third Person of the Trinity, existing in
eternal communion with the Father and the Son. Together with the
Father and the Son, He is to be worshiped and glorified.

We have seen, however, that the Apostles' Creed wants us to see the
Holy Spirit as the One who brings Christ to us. Jesus explained this in
His time celebrating the Passover with His disciples in the Upper
Room before His betrayal by Judas Iscariot in the Garden of
Gethsemane.

What do these passages tell us about the Holy Spirit in relation to
Jesus?

      John 14:16-18

John 15:26

John 16:7

John 16:13-15

Jesus was anointed as the Messiah, the Christ of God, by the Holy Spirit. What role did the Spirit play in the following aspects of Jesus' work as Messiah?

His conception

His baptism

His temptation

His public ministry

His resurrection

What does it mean to say that the Spirit does not work independently in our salvation but in respect to Jesus?

THE BLESSINGS OF THE HOLY SPIRIT

The blessings of the Holy Spirit are the blessings of God the Father secured in the work of Christ. These blessings come to us both individually and in community.

Give a Bible reference and a sentence summarizing each of the following blessings of the Holy Spirit.

New birth

New life

New hope

Some who have turned to Christ for salvation consider their experience rather dull and ordinary. They are convinced their stories don't have the wow-factor of the apostle Paul in Acts 9 or the radical change of those who have lived wicked lives.

But every story of faith in Christ is a miracle. Not just something wonderful and remarkable like the birth of a baby, but a bona fide miracle, super-natural. How do these passages prove that is the case?

Ephesians 2:1-10

1 Corinthians 2:1-14

The Spirit not only works in the individual, He works in *community*. What are some of the ways the Spirit brings Christ to the church that the Creed will lay out?

We closed the last chapter with a prayer from Ephesians that sought to exalt God and expand our appreciation of His manifold blessings of salvation bound up in Jesus Christ. To close this lesson, we turn to Paul's other prayer in Ephesians, this one emphasizing the Spirit's role as conduit of God's grace and power. Paul prays that God…

> … *would grant you, according to the riches of His glory, to be strengthened with might through His Spirit in the inner man, that Christ may dwell in your hearts through faith; that you, being rooted and grounded in love, may be able to comprehend with all the saints what is the width and length and depth and height — to know the love of Christ which passes knowledge; that you may be filled with all the fullness of God. Now to Him who is able to do exceedingly abundantly above all that we ask or think, according to the power that works in us, to Him be glory in the church by Christ Jesus to all generations, forever and ever. Amen. (Eph. 3:16–21)*

Spend time reflecting on this prayer's vocabulary, phrases and concepts. Survey its truth made delightful to Spirit-opened eyes. Note how it lays before believers an impossible task of trying to comprehend a love that is incomprehensible, inviting us to a boundless and lifelong exploration of joy and glory in Christ.

Now pray this prayer, your eyes of faith on the God you seek –the Father Almighty, the Maker of heaven and earth, the God who set His love upon you and sent His Son to save you. Pray for yourself and for your church family.

What questions do you have after reading Chapter 7, "The Holy Spirit," in *The Christian's Creed*?

Chapter 8

THE CHURCH

I believe in ...the holy catholic church,
the communion of saints.

"Church" means different things depending on the context in which the term is used. We go to church on a Sunday morning, meaning the service of worship. Our church may be located in the center of town, referring to the building or meeting place. Each of these is a legitimate usage for communication purposes. But the Creed's use of the word *church* reflects the Bible's emphasis and refers to the people of God.

The Creed uses two terms in particular to describe the church: holy and catholic.

HOLY

1. What are some different ways in which the term *holy* is used in the Bible?

2. How does Daniel serve as an example of holiness?

3. Characterize what each of the following passages from 1 Peter contributes to our understanding of holiness.

   As obedient children, not conforming yourselves to the former lusts, as in your ignorance; but as He who called you is holy, you also be holy in all your conduct, because it is written, "Be holy, for I am holy." (1 Peter 1:14–16)

Coming to Him as to a living stone, rejected indeed by men, but chosen by God and precious, you also, as living stones, are being built up a spiritual house, a holy priesthood, to offer up spiritual sacrifices acceptable to God through Jesus Christ. (1 Peter 2:4–5)

But you are a chosen generation, a royal priesthood, a holy nation, His own special people, that you may proclaim the praises of Him who called you out of darkness into His marvelous light. (1 Peter 2:9)

4. Like perfecting a golf swing, we are called to perfect holiness in the fear of God (2 Cor. 7:1). What does it mean *to perfect holiness* and how does that relate to the *fear* of God?

5. Explain this statement from our book: "The church is holy by the action of God, to be holy by the call of God, and is ultimately holy because the holy God dwells in its midst."

CATHOLIC

Just as "church" can mean different things, so can the word "catholic." In fact, upon hearing *catholic* our minds may go to the Roman Catholic Church and think denominationally. But actually the term leads us away from denominational designation. It speaks to what is distinctive to *all* Christianity. It refers to the people of God throughout the world and across the centuries.

Catholic gives us the perspective that the church is bigger than our local church, and incorporates believers from around the world and across the ages.

To say the church is catholic also reminds us that there is *one* people of God. In what way do the following passages describe this unity?

> *There is one body and one Spirit, just as you were called in one hope of your calling; one Lord, one faith, one baptism; one God and Father of all, who is above all, and through all, and in you all. (Eph. 4:4–6)*

> *The cup of blessing which we bless, is it not the communion of the blood of Christ? The bread which we break, is it not the communion of the body of Christ? For we, though many, are one bread and one body; for we all partake of that one bread. (1 Cor. 10:16–17)*

COMMUNION OF SAINTS

1. By what names do these New Testament letters address believers: 2 Cor. 1:1, Phil. 1:1, 1 Pet. 1:1-2, Jude 1?

2. What does it mean to be a *saint*?

3. *Communion* means to have something in common. This can be seen in the Greek word *koinonia*. What are some ways *koinonia* can be translated?

The life of Christ's church is bound up in the life of Jesus Christ. Believers (or saints) individually and together *partake* of His benefits, *partner* in His mission, and *participate* in His body. In partaking, we *share in* Christ's blessings, such as forgiveness of sins and hope of eternal life. In partnering we *join together* in the mission Jesus has for us to be salt and light in this world. In participating we *involve ourselves* in His body, serving synergistically and energetically with the gifts the Spirit has given us. Together we exercise the "one another" passages of the Bible, such as building one another up, encouraging one another, bearing one another's burdens, and all those other passages that describe the dynamic body life of Christ's church.

What do the following passages tell us about believers' communion with Christ and with one another?

I, therefore, the prisoner of the Lord, beseech you to walk worthy of the calling with which you were called, with all lowliness and gentleness, with longsuffering, bearing with one another in love, endeavoring to keep the unity of the Spirit in the bond of peace. (Ephesians 4:1–3)

There are diversities of gifts, but the same Spirit. There are differences of ministries, but the same Lord. And there are diversities of activities, but it is the same God who works all in all. But the manifestation of the Spirit is given to each one for the profit of all...

For as the body is one and has many members, but all the members of that one body, being many, are one body, so also is Christ. For by one Spirit we were all baptized into one body—whether Jews or Greeks, whether slaves or free—and have all been made to drink into one Spirit. (1 Corinthians 12:4-7, 12–13)

Sometimes communion is expressed as *fellowship*. Fellowship is not just social time; it is the living out of the bond of the Spirit in participation in Christ (1 Cor. 10:16-17). The writer of the letter to the Hebrews speaks of the importance of involvement in one another's lives for protection and spiritual growth. How do we see this mutual responsibility in the passages below?

> *Beware, brethren, lest there be in any of you an evil heart of unbelief in departing from the living God; but exhort one another daily, while it is called "Today," lest any of you be hardened through the deceitfulness of sin. For we have become partakers of Christ if we hold the beginning of our confidence steadfast to the end. (Heb. 3:12–14)*

> *And let us consider one another in order to stir up love and good works, not forsaking the assembling of ourselves together, as is the manner of some, but exhorting one another, and so much the more as you see the Day approaching. (Heb. 10:24–25)*

If you have professed faith in Jesus Christ, His design is for you to be part of a local church. The church is an incubator for Christian maturity and an outpost for kingdom mission.

What questions do you have after reading Chapter 8, "The Church," in *The Christian's Creed*?

Chapter 9

THE FORGIVENESS OF SINS

I believe in … the forgiveness of sins.

This chapter in our book begins: "The Apostles' Creed now turns to the blessings of salvation in Christ, summed up in the forgiveness of sins and eternal life, blessings shared by the communion of saints." Through faith in Christ, believers are blessed as ones acquitted, accepted, and assured of eternal glory.

Complete the following statement from our book: "Forgiveness of sin brings us to the crux of the gospel and the beating heart of the church as the redeemed of the Lord.

The church is a _____ of those forgiven, of those who

_____ forgiveness, and of those who _____

forgiveness."

FORGIVENESS

Outlining a book of the Bible by its chapters usually works quite well. In outlining the book of Romans, however, we would miss a critical division were we to rely on the chapter breaks. That watershed moment is found the junction of Romans 3:20 and 21.

　1.　Read Romans 3:19-20. What do these verses say about our ability to save ourselves by our own efforts at keeping God's law?

　2.　Read Romans 3:21-26. What did God do that we could not?

The "but now" of Romans 3:21 sends us in an entirely different direction to look for salvation. It empties us of ability to save ourselves and brings us to rest fully and only on God's provision in Jesus Christ. Not what *we* did, but what *He* did – precisely what the Apostles' Creed emphasizes.

Earlier in Romans 3 Paul paints a bleak picture of guilt and impotence – all have sinned, all are guilty, all stand condemned. The question is, how can we be forgiven of the debt of our sin against a holy God? The rest of Romans 3 gives us the answer.

1. Where do we find God's gift of forgiveness in the book of Romans, even though we might not find the word itself?

2. What other than forgiveness of sins is necessary for our acceptance by God?

3. Complete: In Christ, our sin is not simply _____; it is _____.

4. By grace through faith, the believer stands _____ by Christ's redeeming blood and _____ in Christ's spotless righteousness.

PRACTICING FORGIVENESS

By faith in Christ, we stand justified. That means *every* sin – past, present and future, public or private, big or little, thought about or acted upon – is accounted for and forgiven, paid for through the sacrifice of Jesus Christ on our behalf. In addition, Christ's righteousness, His perfect record of law-keeping, is credited to us.

But we continue to sin. A holy life is a struggle for us. God knows that and He ministers His grace to us.

Read 1 John 1:5-10

1. Who is John writing to, believers or unbelievers? How do you know?

2. Admitting we continue to sin actually indicates we are Christians. How can we conclude this from 1 John 5:13?

3. What does it mean to *confess* sin?

4. Why does John say that God is faithful and *just* to forgive us our sin rather than faithful and *merciful*?

Read 1 John 2:1-2

1. Why does God's assured forgiveness not encourage us to sin? See also Romans 6:1-2.

2. In what way is Jesus our Advocate with the Father when we sin?

3. What does it mean for Jesus to be the *propitiation* for our sins?

4. Why do you think Jesus is called "the righteous" in this context?

5. Forgiveness of sin is found not in mere confession of _____ but in confession of _____.

6. What does verse 2 tell us about any way of salvation other than Jesus?

How does the forgiveness of sins we declare in the third section of the Apostles' Creed relate to the second section of the Creed?

PROCLAIMING FORGIVENESS

1. What does it mean that the holy catholic church is in the business of proclaiming forgiveness? (Luke 24:46-47; Acts 10:43; 13:38-39; 26:18)

2. How does the church demonstrate forgiveness as a witness to the world? (Eph. 4:1-3, 29-32)

3. How does the celebration of the sacrament of the Lord's Supper remind us of God's forgiveness, as well as remind us of our call to practice and proclaim that forgiveness?

What is your favorite song to celebrate God's forgiveness? Write out the words that you find especially meaningful to you.

What questions do you have after reading Chapter 9, "The Forgiveness of Sins," in *The Christian's Creed*?

Chapter 10

RESURRECTION TO LIFE EVERLASTING

I believe in ...the resurrection of the body,
and the life everlasting.

Jesus regularly lifted people's eyes to a better life – a life abundant and eternal, free from the scourge of sin. In the face of death and despair, Jesus said, "Take heart, I have overcome" (John 16:33). He invites people to look to Him that they might overcome by faith in Him.

> *I am the resurrection and the life. He who believes in Me, though he may die, he shall live. And whoever lives and believes in Me shall never die. Do you believe this? (John 11:25–26)*

To the Samaritan woman at the well (John 4:13-14) He offered eternal life. He spoke of Himself as the bread of life, of whom to partake by faith would bring life eternal (John 6:52-58). In speaking of the Holy Spirit, Jesus issued this promise: "If anyone thirsts, let him come to Me and drink. He who believes in Me, as the Scripture has said, out of his heart will flow rivers of living water" (John 7:37–38).

Because Jesus lives, those who trust in Him need not fear death. Death is an equal opportunity destroyer but to those who rest in Christ by faith Jesus says: "Do not be afraid; I am the First and the Last. I am He who lives, and was dead, and behold, I am alive forevermore. Amen. And I have the keys of Hades and of Death" (Rev 1:17–18).

God regularly speaks to us in the distress of this life to remind us that our bodies are but fragile vessels of clay inhabited by eternal glory (2 Cor. 4:16-18), and that we have an inheritance in heaven secured by Jesus (John 14:1-3). That inheritance is reserved for us and we are preserved for it (1 Pet. 1:3-9). The sufferings of this life are mitigated by the hope to come: "For I consider that the sufferings of this present time are not worthy to be compared with the glory which shall be revealed in us" (Romans 8:18).

God's plan for those who look to His Son for salvation, who rest in what He did, what only He could do, as the Creed lays out, is that such will live in full and uninterrupted fellowship with Him in the new heavens and new earth. Moreover, that existence will not be as disembodied spirits but with a resurrection body that is part of the new creation.

It is with these glorious redemption realities that the Apostles' Creed leaves us. Our declaration of faith ends on a high note, the highest note possible.

RESURRECTION OF THE BODY

1. What assurance does Jesus offer in John 6:40?

2. Read 1 Corinthians 15:35-58

    a. What is contrasted with "flesh and blood"? How does Jesus' conversation with Nicodemus in John 3:3-6 reinforce this contrast?

    b. What does Paul mean by "spiritual body"?

    c. How is our mortal body different from our resurrection body?

    d. How will *our* resurrection bodies correspond to *Jesus'* resurrection body?

3. According to Romans 8:9-11 and 8:23, what role does the Holy Spirit play in Christ's resurrection and ours?

LIFE EVERLASTING

The Bible gives us a taste of the wonders of eternal life. It also gives us a glimpse of eternal death. Jesus taught frequently about hell, not the realm of the departed as the Creed references (Hades) but as a place of punishment in satisfaction of divine justice (Gehenna).

1. How do passages like Matthew 10:28, 2 Thessalonians 1:7-10, and Revelation 20:13-15 describe eternal death?

2. Against the backdrop of eternal death, what comfort does God extend for those who trust in Christ? See 2 Thess. 2:16-17, Jude 24-25.

How does the story of the Bottle Dungeon in our book convey the horrors of hell?

The Book of Revelation uses exotic images and wondrous signs and sumptuous feasts to tantalize us with the glories in store for those who love God, those who by grace alone, through faith alone, in Christ alone have been made heirs of eternal life. But all this pales in respect to Jesus' summary of eternal life.

1. How does Jesus describe eternal life in John 17:3?

2. In what way is Jesus' description the ultimate glory of God's saving purpose for us?

3. How can that eternal life be ours? See John 3:16, 5:24, 10:28, 17:2.

The apostle Paul closes his second letter to the Corinthians with this benediction: "The grace of the Lord Jesus Christ, and the love of God, and the communion of the Holy Spirit be with you all. Amen" (2 Cor. 13:14). How is this benediction similar to the Apostles' Creed in its emphasis that salvation is Trinitarian?

Lay the Apostles' Creed before you. Read it through slowly, reflecting on each phrase. Read it again, out loud, owning each declaration by faith, savoring it as you would rich food. Review it once more, this time as a *prayer* to the God of your salvation – Father, Son, and Holy Spirit.

What questions do you have after reading Chapter 10, "Resurrection to Life Everlasting," in *The Christian's Creed?*

EXCURSUS

Christian Living

For centuries Christians have joined their voices in reciting the Apostles' Creed. The Creed has served to catechize in the Christian faith, to confess that faith through its declarations, to unite in kindred faith for corporate worship, and to call unbelievers to faith in the faith.

The Apostles' Creed disciples in the gospel. It lays out a syllabus for study of the Christian faith. It proclaims a redemption grounded in the triune God and centered in the person and work of Jesus Christ. To embrace the Creed is to ascribe all glory to God for such a great salvation.

But does the Apostles' Creed speak to morality? Does it address the social issues of our day and those of generations past and future? Do the words "I believe" affect the stand we take regarding areas related to Christian living?

The answer is no, and yes. The Creed does not explicitly speak to social issues or to any issues of morality for that matter. But it does speak emphatically to *where* we find God's direction and *why* we look to Him as disciples of Jesus Christ.

The Apostles' Creed provides three considerations for determining what we believe and how we live.

THE TRUTH "I BELIEVE"

In arriving at what we believe, we are not left to our own imaginations, preferences, or sensibilities. The formulations of the Creed are not innovative; they are derivative. The Creed follows the lead of Paul's preaching to the Corinthians:

For I delivered to you as of first importance what I also received: that Christ died for our sins in accordance with the Scriptures, that he was buried, that

*he was raised on the third day in accordance with the Scriptures (1 Cor.
15:3–4, emphasis added).*

The Apostles' Creed directs us to an authority outside of ourselves. It
lifts our eyes to God and leads us to look for the sanction of "thus says
the Lord" in the positions we take and in the way we conduct our lives.
"I believe" is a response to what God reveals in His written Word.

CHRIST AS "LORD"

The Creed emphasizes the lordship of Jesus Christ. He is the One to
whom all authority has been given. That authority is kingdom
authority. It is exhibited in redemptive life that consecrates all of life to
God (Col. 3:17; 1 Cor. 10:31) and lives that life in resurrection power
(Phil. 4:13; Eph. 1:19).

Those who have been delivered from the kingdom of darkness and
enfolded into the kingdom of Christ, who have bowed the knee before
Him by God's grace are "to walk in a manner worthy of the Lord, fully
pleasing to him: bearing fruit in every good work and increasing in the
knowledge of God" (Col. 1:10; compare Col. 2:6).

If we call Christ "Lord," it is incumbent upon us that we do what He
says. That means our opinions and options are to be brought under the
lordship of Jesus Christ, hearing His word and putting it into practice.
Saints are to live sanctified lives (1 Cor. 1:2; Matt. 7:24-25).

THE CHURCH AS "HOLY"

When we say we believe in a "holy" church, we understand ourselves
to be a people *in* the world but not *of* the world (John 17:14-19), a
people separated unto God, indwelt by the Holy Spirit.

The church is where the kingdom of God and His Christ is most visible.
The church is where disciples are gathered and taught to obey (Mt.
28:18-20). Believers are educated, equipped, encouraged, and engaged

to seek first the kingdom of God with its counter-cultural perspectives, priorities, values, ethics, commitments, and goals. Our positions and practices should be kingdom-qualified.

****

So when it comes to how we live, the Creed does not so much give us bread as it teaches us how to bake bread—by the light and heat of God's Word, in His call to be holy unto Him, through living under the lordship of Jesus Christ. Christ gives us this reminder as His holy catholic church: "For at one time you were darkness, but now you are light in the Lord. Walk as children of light (for the fruit of light is found in all that is good and right and true), and try to discern what is pleasing to the Lord" (Eph. 5:8–10).

Made in the USA
Las Vegas, NV
19 March 2021

19828957R00042